Positive Vibes Only

BY JEFFREY PICKLES

POSITIVE VIBES ONLY

IF YOU NEVER TRY

YOU'LL NEVER KNOW...

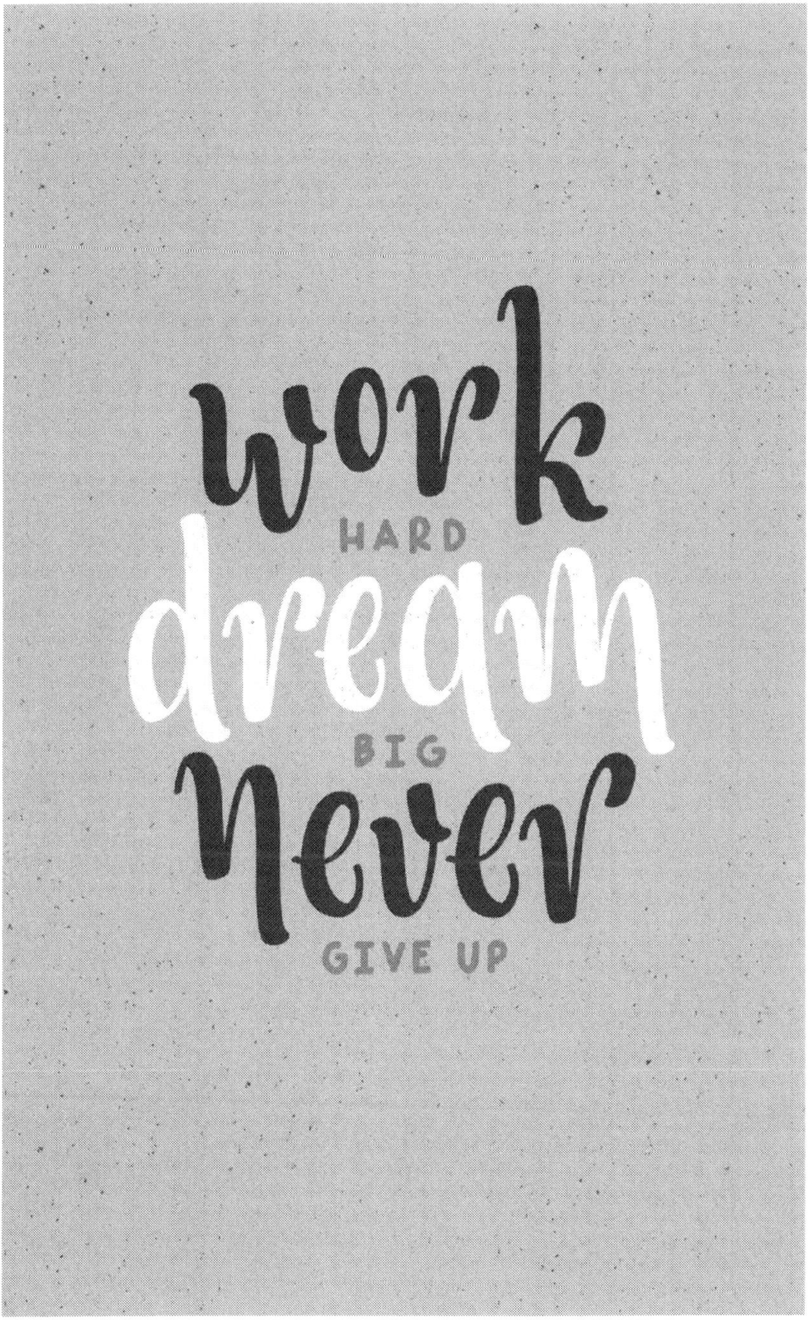
work
HARD
dream
BIG
never
GIVE UP

Inspiration

EXISTS

BUT IT HAS TO

FIND YOU WORKING

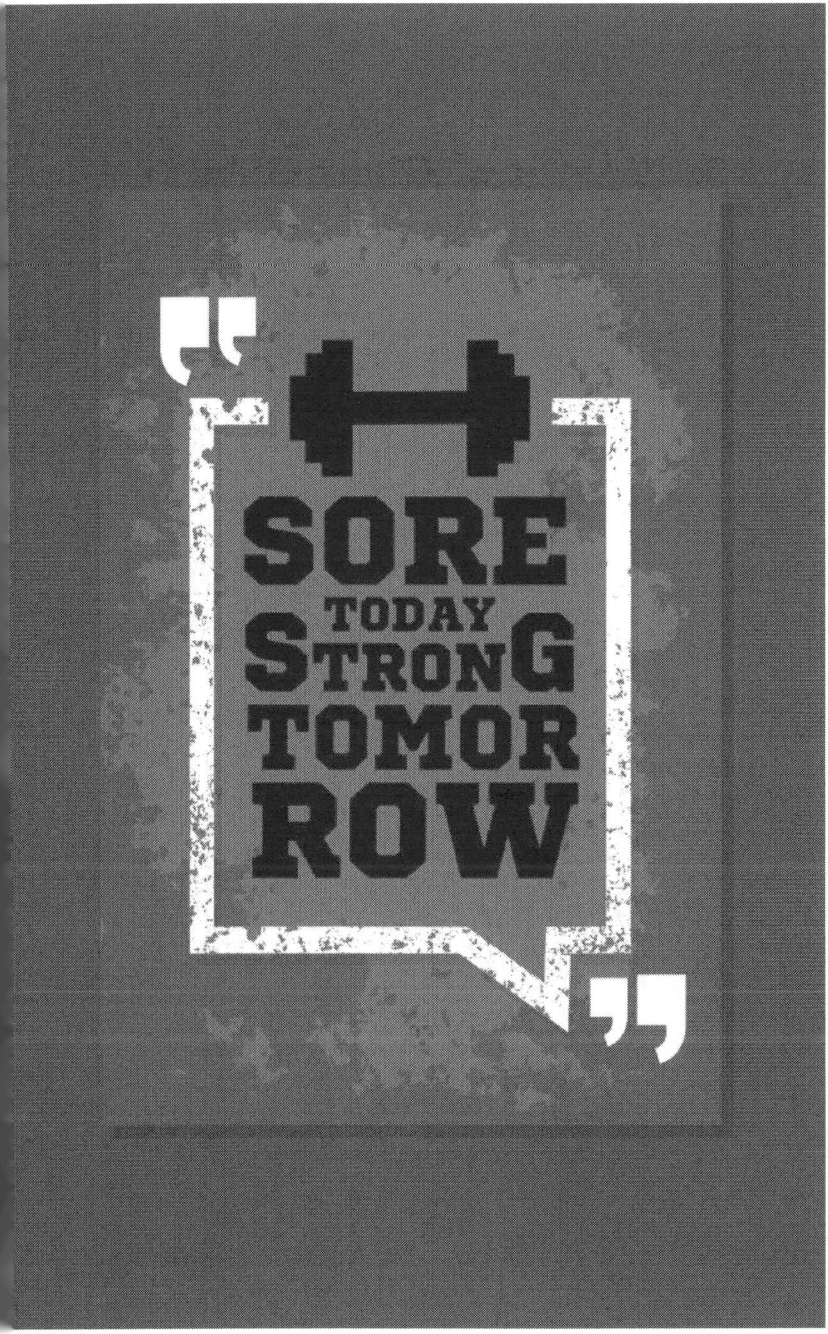
SORE
TODAY
STRONG
TOMOR
ROW

life
IS AN
adventure
BE AN
explorer

Everything
YOU WANT
(is) on THE **OTHER**
SIDE of fear

your
ONLY
limit
— IS YOU —

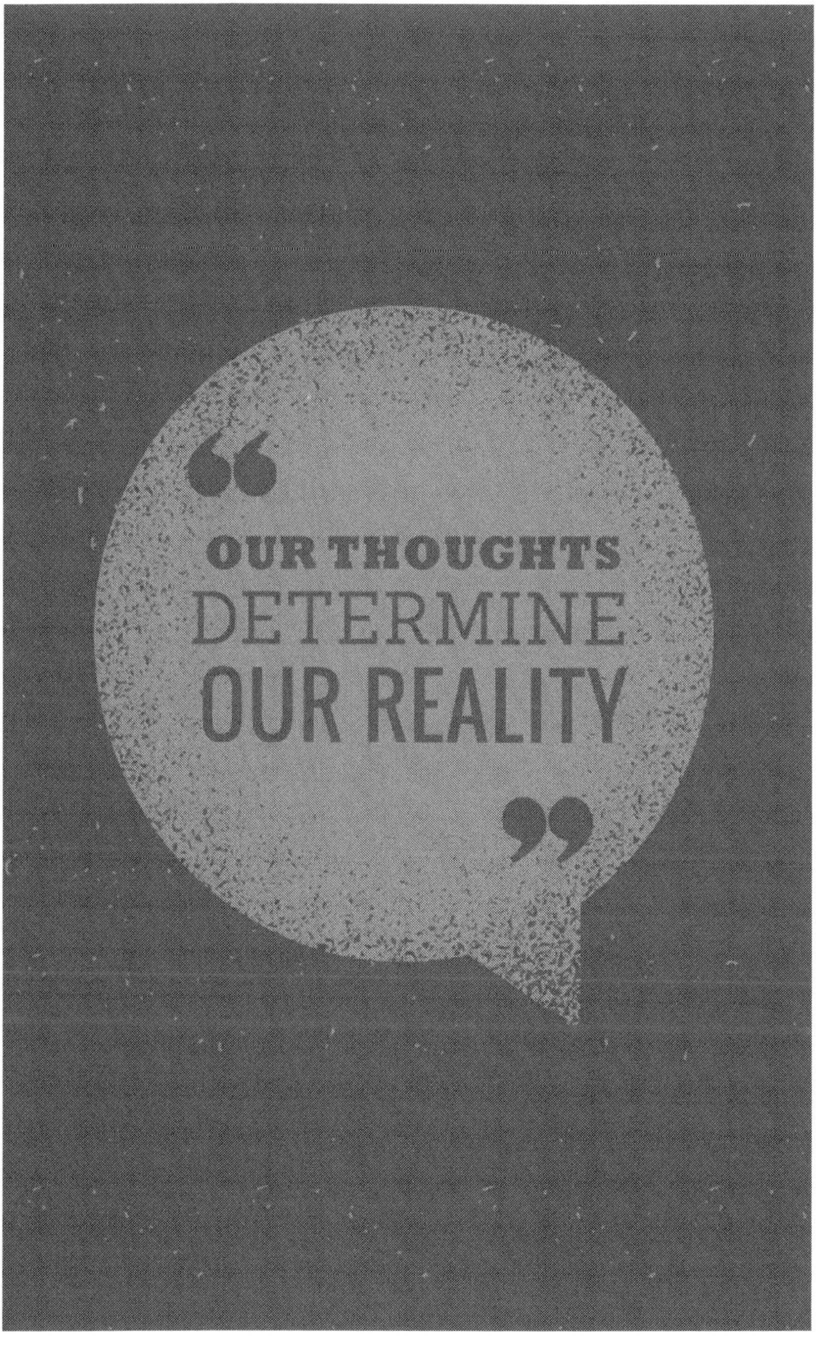
OUR THOUGHTS
DETERMINE
OUR REALITY

.

The
IMAGINATION
IS THE *eye*
OF THE SOUL

Cinderella

IS PROOF THAT

a new pair of

Shoes

CAN CHANGE

Your life

Never say Never

BE THE

best

version

of you

DO IT WITH Passion OR NOT AT ALL

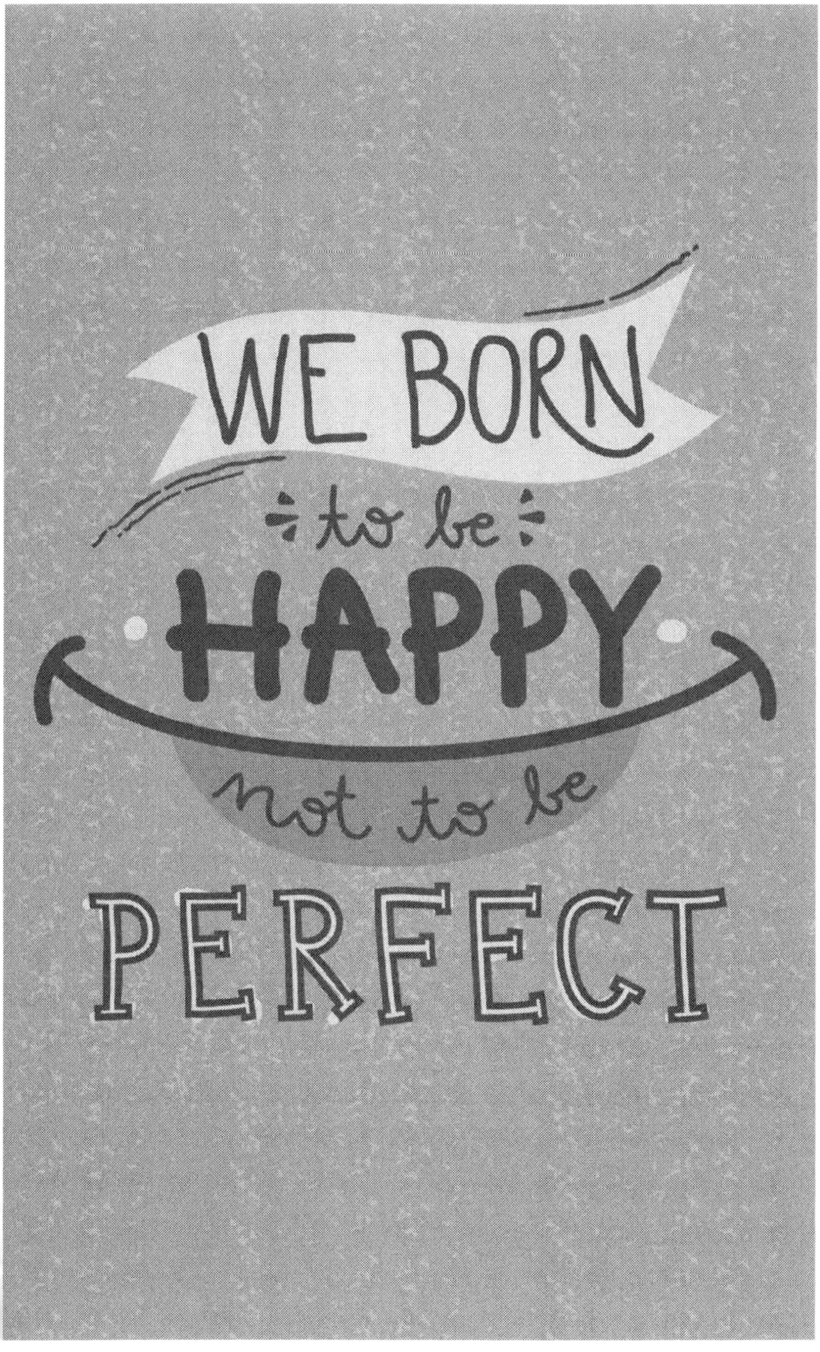
WE BORN
to be
HAPPY
not to be
PERFECT

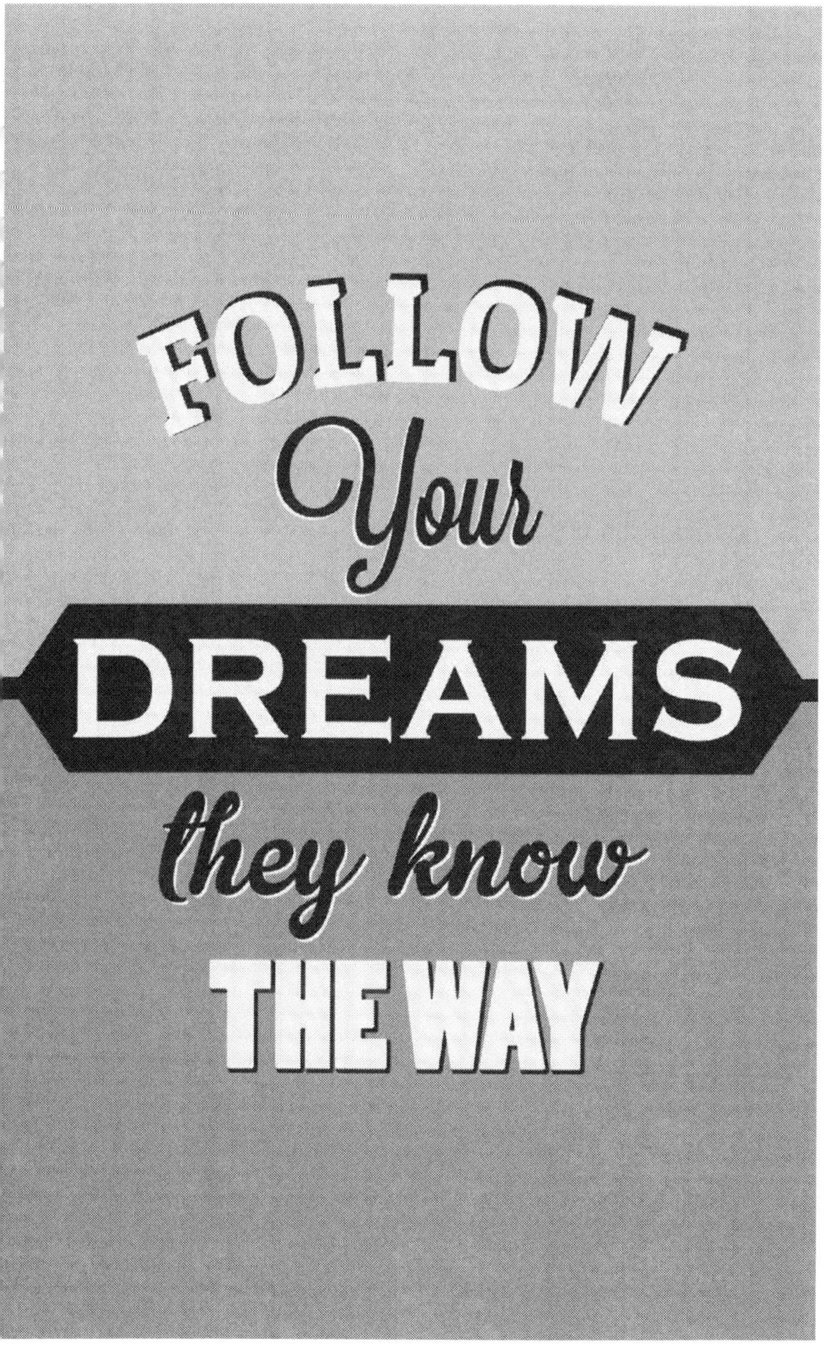
FOLLOW
Your
DREAMS
they know
THE WAY

BE PROUD
of who
YOU
ARE

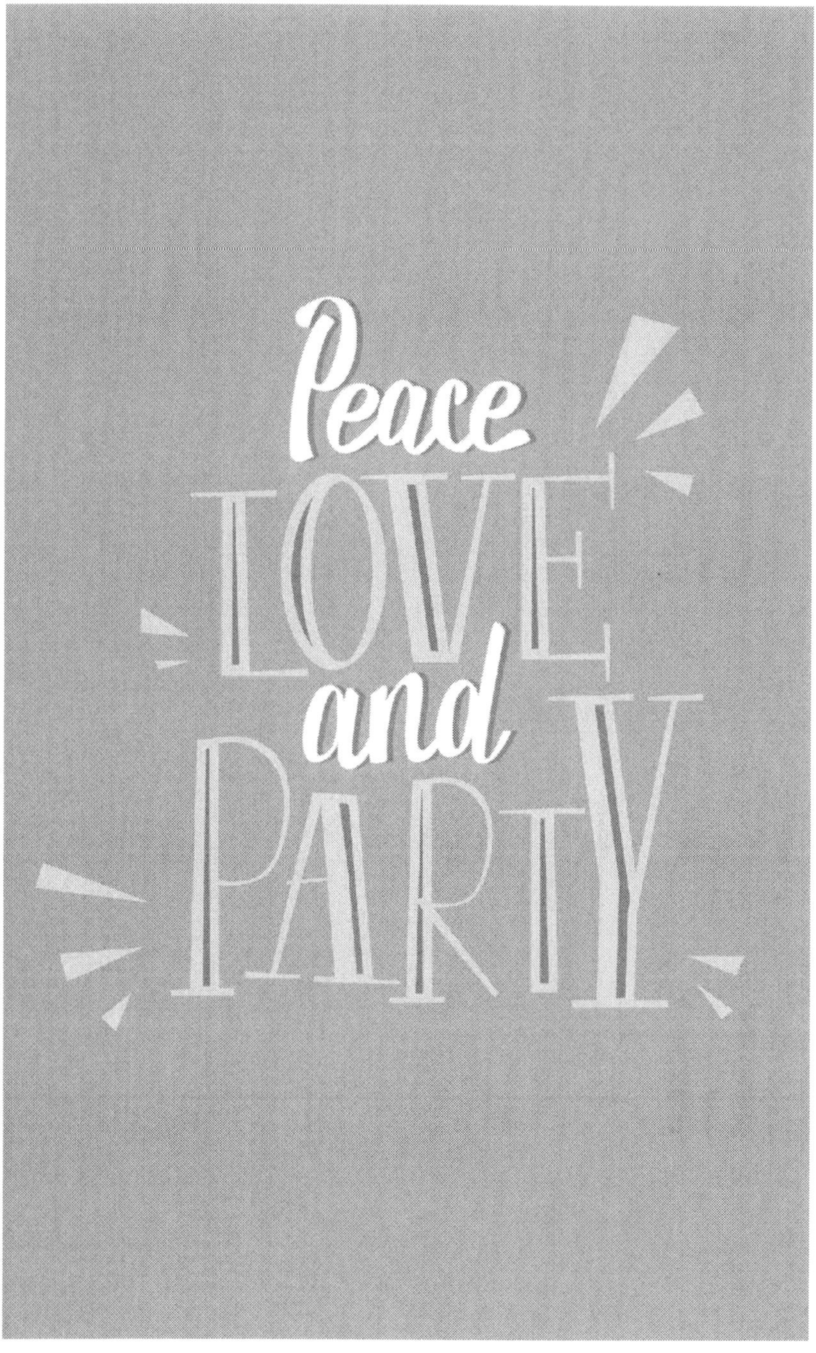
Peace
LOVE
and
PARTY

Creativity

≈ is ≈

INTELLIGENCE

Having fun

LIFE IS BETTER

in running shoes

It's just
a bad day,
Not
a bad life

ALWAYS

Start

YOUR   DAY

smiling

FEAR
· · · OF · · ·
FAILING
◄ IS A ►
DISTRACTION
► MORE ◄
· · THAN · ·
ANYTHING

THE ONLY WAY

⋸ TO DO ⋸

Great Work

IS TO

Love

WHAT YOU DO

Failure
– IS –
Success
IN
Progress

EVERYTHING
YOU CAN
IMAGINE
IS
REAL

Kindness

—CHANGES—

Everything

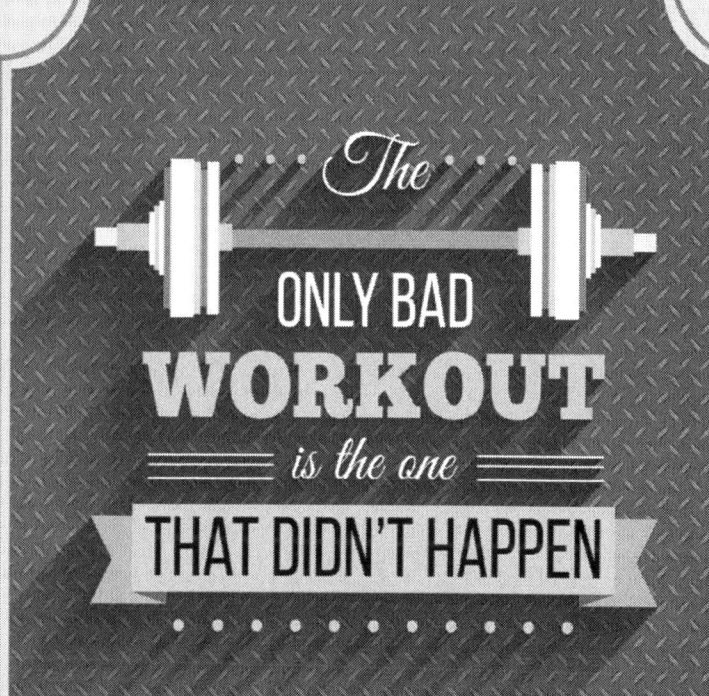

LOGIC WILL
GET YOU FROM
A to B
imagination TAKE YOU
EVERYWHERE

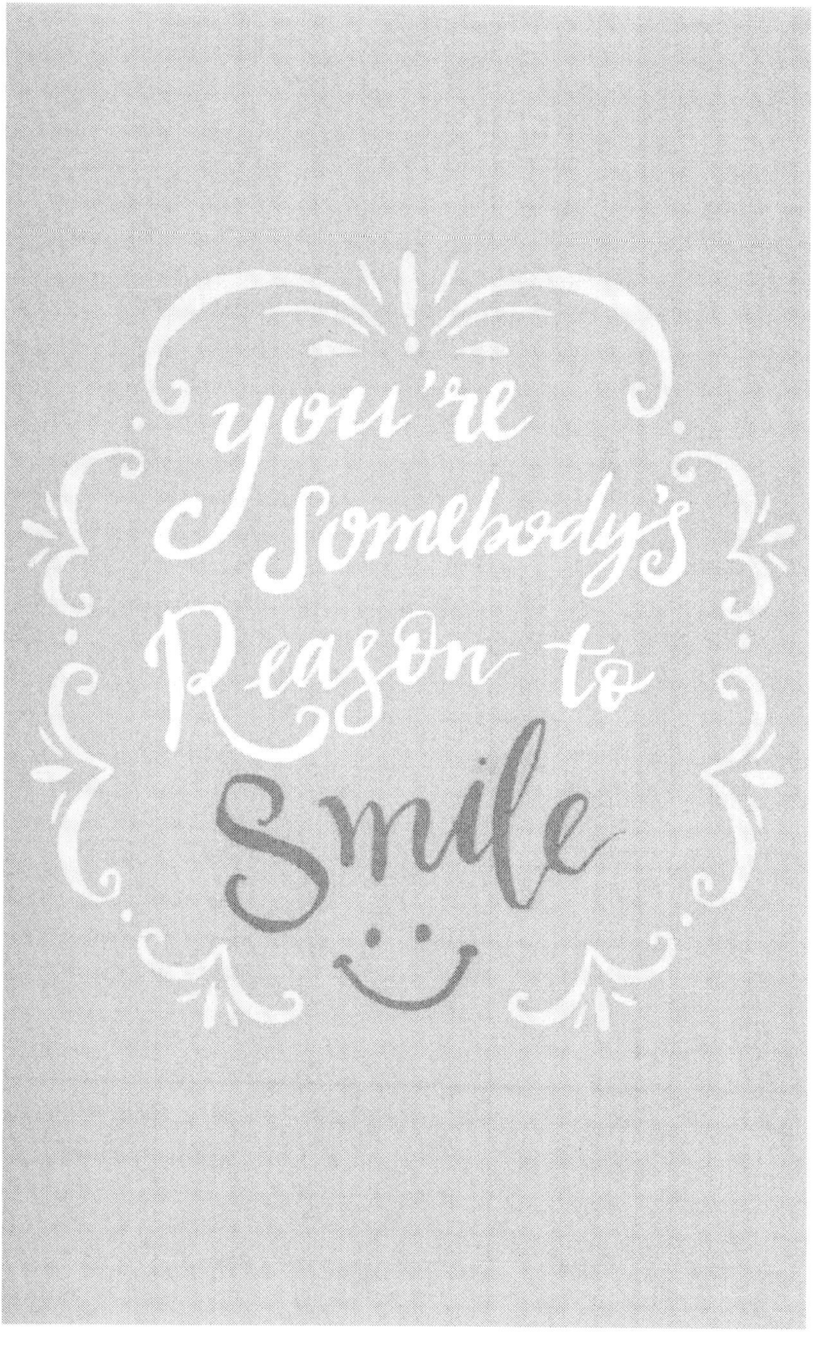
you're
Somebody's
Reason to
Smile

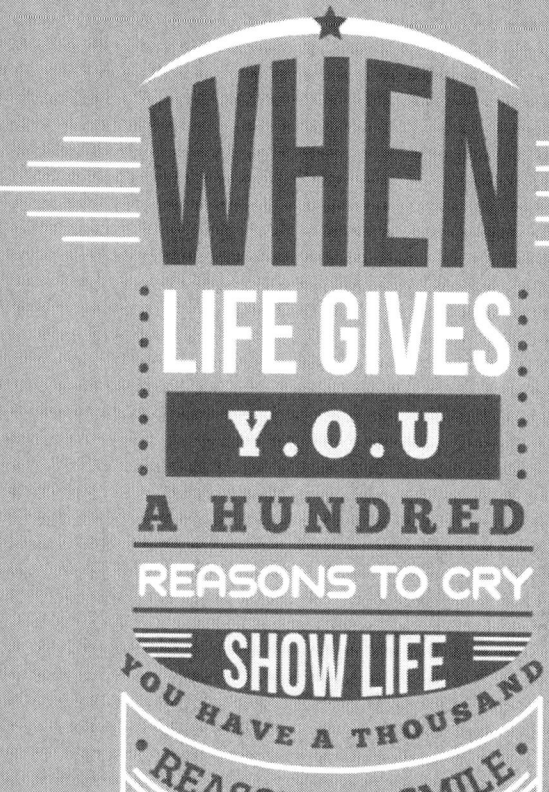

MAGIC

is

►SOMETHING◄

YOU MAKE

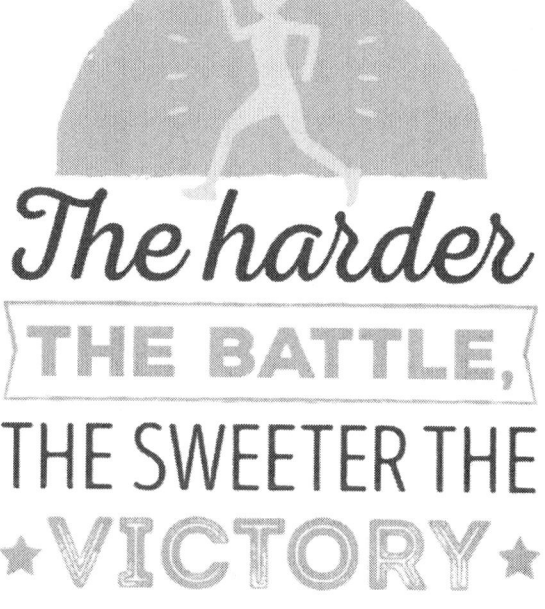

The harder THE BATTLE, THE SWEETER THE ★ VICTORY ★

Stay humble
WORK HARD
be kind
♥

DON'T LET

THE PAST

STEAL YOUR

PRESENT

ENJOY

THE

LITTLE

THINGS

THE **HARDER** you work THE **LUCKIER** you get

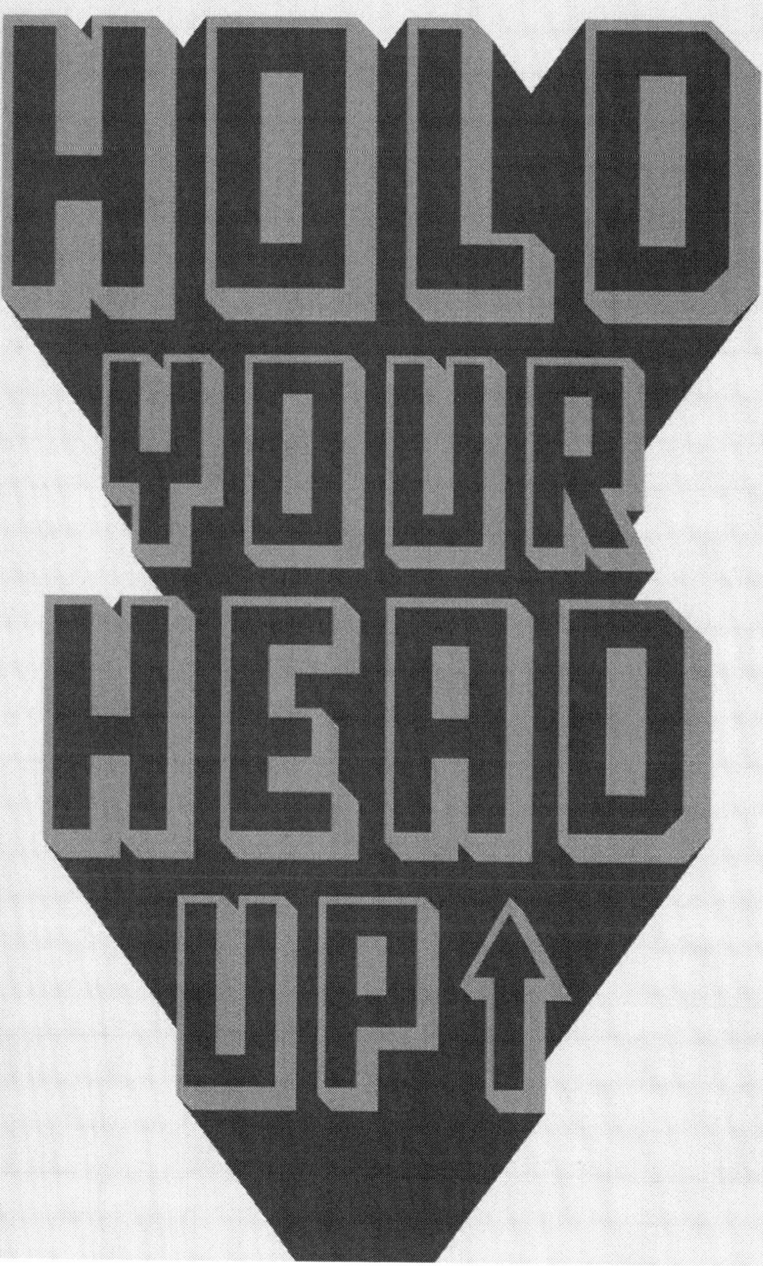
HOLD
YOUR
HEAD
UP

Wake up
and be
awesome

DIFFICULT
roads
LEAD TO
beautiful
DESTINATIONS

THE HEART
THAT
Loves
IS
ALWAYS
Young

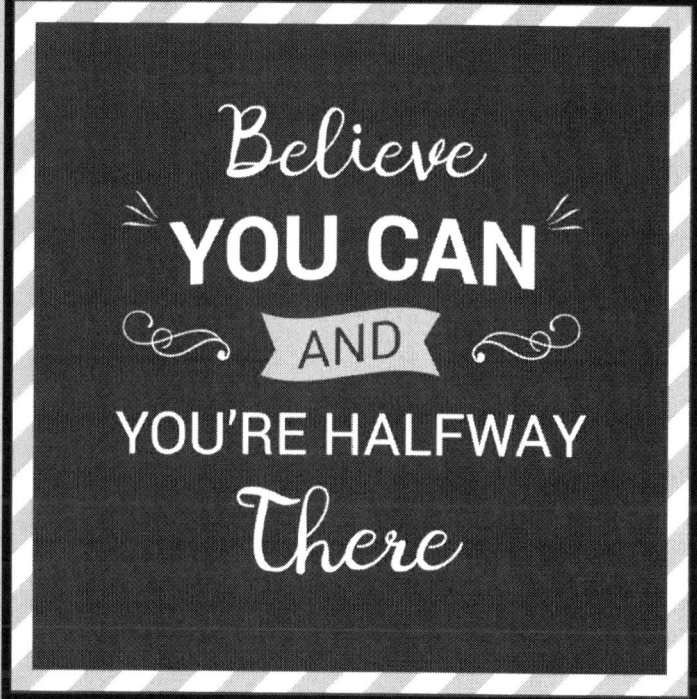

Thank you

More books by this author:

ADULTS ARE THE DUMIST

KIDS ARE THE FUNNIEST

STUDENT QUIBBLES AND QUERIES (A HOGWARTS LIBRARY BOOK)

YOU'LL NEVER GUESS WHAT I JUST OVERHEARD!

ACKNOWLEDGEMENTS

Images used from the following sources;

1) Freepix
2) Artmonkey
3) Balasoiu
4) Freepix
5) Freepix
6) Freepix
7) Freepix
8) Freepix
9) kjpargeter
10) Freepix
11) Designerhrenov
12) Balasoiu
13) Freepix
14) Starline
15) Freepix
16) Freepix
17) Winkimages
18) Freepix
19) Freepix
20) Freepix
21) Eightonesix, Freepix
22) Freepix
23) Freepix
24) Freepix
25) Freepix
26) Winkimages
27) Freepix
28) Freepix
29) Freepix

30) Freepix

31) 0melapics, Freepix

32) Balasoiu, Freepix

33) Freepix

34) Artmonkey, Freepix

35) AndyleCr, freepix

36) Lesyaskripak, freepix

37) Freepix

38) Artmonkey, freepix

39) Freepix

40) Freepix

41) Freepix

42) Freepix

43) Freepix

44) Freepix

45) Freepix

46) Freepix

47) Freepix

48) Eightonesix

49) Freepix

50) Freepix

51) Balasoiu

52) Kjpargeter

53) Artmonkey

54) Artmonkey

55) balasoiu

56) freepix

57) winkimages

58) freepix

59) freepix

60) starline

Printed in Great
Britain
by Amazon